The emergence of early newspaper print in colonial Calcutta. (1780-1820)

Snippets from a hybrid world: grammar books, politics and advertisements.

Tapati Bharadwaj

Copyright © 2013 Tapati Bharadwaj

All rights reserved.

ISBN:8192875202
ISBN-13: 978-81-928752-0-0

DEDICATION

To the hope that even after tomorrow, we do not forget the nature of how printed works from the West entered India. We open books, turn pages, and read voraciously, as if to satisfy an insatiable hunger.

CONTENTS

Acknowledgments — i

1 On the arrival of print in Calcutta: a brief foray into how an epistemic shift took place. — 1

2 Reading news in Calcutta, circa 1780 or so: war, politics and habits of consumption in the realm of imperial print. — 8

3 How natives learnt about print. — 29

4 Some concluding thoughts on early print. — 32

Works Cited — 37

LIST OF FIGURES

1. Figure 1: Title page of Halhed's Grammar book. — 2
2. Figure 2: Habits of consumption; advertisements. — 13
3. Figure 3: Habits of consumption; more advertisements. — 14
4. Figure 4: Summaries from six month old British newspapers. — 16
5. Figure 5: Extracts from State Papers. — 18
6. Figure 6: Foreign news. — 19
7. Figure 7: Letter written by Cornwallis to the Secretary of State about the Mysore wars. — 21
8. Figure 8: Official treaty between Cornwallis and Tipu Sultan. — 23
9. Figure 9: Public entry of the captive princes. — 24
10. Figure 10: A multilingual text. — 27

Tapati Bharadwaj

ACKNOWLEDGMENTS

··· ··· ··· ···

1 ON THE ARRIVAL OF PRINT IN CALCUTTA: A BRIEF FORAY INTO HOW AN EPISTEMIC SHIFT TOOK PLACE.

Nathaniel Halhed's grammar book, *A Grammar of the Bengal language*,[1] was printed in 1778, and was one of the first printed texts in India. It had a multilingual title page: it had a Bengali subtitle alongside the English title (and Roman numericals at the bottom), making it undoubtedly a first of its kind (fig.1). The grammar book was targeting an English readership located both in India and in England. The advent of print in colonial Bengal in the last two decades of the eighteenth century is a story that has its beginnings far away from its source of production. Print technology developed in the western world and was carried across to Calcutta as a by product of colonization and the efforts of the East India Company. If the natives were to trust the Britishers, and be complicit partners, they had to believe that the rulers were present for their own good and happiness. A realm of print culture developed that was extremely sophisticated in its use of technology and the manner in which it was conceptualized by the Britishers. Initially, both native and English texts were meant to be consumed by the Britishers, as is evident in the book above, but subsequent native use was implied. Close interaction between the natives and the Englishmen would allow the natives to understand how print worked and they would inevitably want to learn about it.

---

[1] Nathaniel Brassey Halhed, *A Grammar of the Bengal Language*. Hooghly in Bengal, 1778. Reprint. (ed.) R. C. Alston (England: The Scolar Press Ltd., 1969).

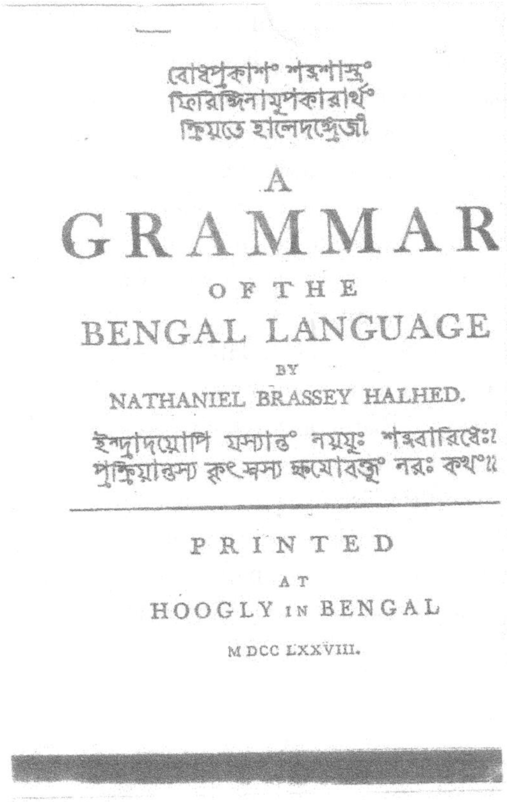

বোধপ্রকাশং শব্দশাস্ত্রং
ফিরিঙ্গিনামুপকারার্থং
ক্রিয়তে হালেদঙ্গ্রেজী

A
GRAMMAR
OF THE
BENGAL LANGUAGE
BY
NATHANIEL BRASSEY HALHED.

ইন্দ্রাদয়োপি যস্যান্তং নযযুঃ শব্দবারিধেঃ।
প্রক্রিয়ান্তস্য কৃৎস্নস্য ক্ষমোবক্তুং নরঃ কথং॥

PRINTED
AT
HOOGLY IN BENGAL
MDCC LXXVIII.

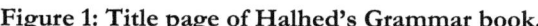

Figure 1: Title page of Halhed's Grammar book.

The emergence of early newspaper print in colonial Calcutta.

My work on print in colonial Bengal can also be described as the "social and cultural history of communication by print";[2] according to Robert Darnton, the purpose of such studies is to understand how ideas were communicated by print, and how these ideas and books came into contact with society and affected the thoughts of the society they spread in. All printed books, Darnton writes, generally pass through the same "life cycle" which is also a "communications circuit" that runs from the author, to the publisher, the printer, the shipper, the bookseller, and the reader."[3] The "communication circuit" in the early phases of print culture in Calcutta, that is pre-1800, catered to the specific needs of the Britishers. The booksellers, writers and printers were English. That is, prior to the turn of the century, the realm of print culture was a closed circuit -- all books, newspapers, gazettes, legal translations, in fact, all printed material had a very specific readership and catered to the practical, aesthetic and intellectual needs of the Europeans.

It is, therefore, not at all ironic that the first book to be printed in Bengal, India, Nathaniel Halhed's *A Grammar of the Bengal Language* (1778), was under the patronage of the East India Company and meant for a British readership. The book was printed in Hooghly, made its way to England and sold in London by Elmsley. In 1783, a review in an English journal, *A New Review,* described the book as "classical" and of much use to those Britishers who traveled to India to work in "public departments," allowing for better "correspondence" between the natives and the rulers.[4] The need for communication was but one of the reasons as to why the book was praised; the Bengali "characters" are "beautiful," the reviewer wrote, and would arouse the curiosity of the British reader. Letterpress technology had captured the "exotic" beauty of the Bengali script, revealing the apparent mastery of western print mechanization over scribal manuscripts.

---

[2] Robert Darnton. "What is the History of Books," *The Book History Reader.* ed. David Finkelstein and Alistair McCleery. (London and NY: Routledge, 2003), pp. 9-26.

[3] Ibid., p. 11.

[4] "Review of A Grammar of the Bengal Language," *A New Review*. Vol. III. 1783, pp. 156-157.

Tapati Bharadwaj

In order to print a multilingual text, native types were needed, and so were printing presses. Charles Wilkins, a twenty eight year old writer with the East India Company, was requested by the then Governor General Warren Hastings to come up with Bengali types which were used to print Halhed's book in Hooghly. I am not sure as to what a printing press would be doing in Hooghly, unless it was an isolated instance of printing being done in a port where British presence would have been inevitable. Printing was not an easy task; for example, in the absence of paper mills, most of the paper was imported: two types of paper were available – Indian handmade paper, also called Patna paper and the more expensive imported paper. William Carey's paper mill was built around 1800 but there were also efforts taken to build paper mills before.[5]

Till as recently as two hundred years ago, India was a manuscript culture meaning that the printed text did not exist. When the transition took place from a manuscript culture to a print one, it seems to have taken place with great ease, implying that the shift was made without much murmurs and complaints from at least the native, elite sections of society. The Britishers, on the other hand, at seeing the beautiful manuscripts in Indian languages must have been reminded of their pre-print past and a lot of care was taken to ensure that these manuscripts were well kept. When Tipu Sultan lost the Mysore wars (1780-90s), his library was also taken and a concern was raised by the Company soldiers as to how the manuscripts were to be kept safe: "That part of the library of the late Tippoo Sultan, which was presented by the army to the Court of Directors, is lately arrived in Bengal; the Governor-General strongly recommends that the Oriental manuscripts composing this collection, should be deposited in the library of the College of Fort William, and it is his intention to retain the manuscripts accordingly, until he shall receive the orders of the Court upon the subject."[6] There was no rampant erasure of the Indian manuscript past, and in fact, the Company was keen to preserve this aspect of Indian culture.

---

[5] For more see Graham Shaw, *Printing in Calcutta to 1800* (London: The Bibliographical Society, 1981), pp. 28-39.

[6] "Introduction," in *The Annals of the College of Fort William, from the Period of its Foundation*. Arranged and Published by Thomas Roebuck, Calcutta (Printed by Philip Periera at the Hindoostanee Press, 1819),

The emergence of early newspaper print in colonial Calcutta.

Were the Indians happy at the advent of print technology and did they understand the epistemic shift that would take place at the introduction of print? When we consider how print did impact what was essentially a manuscript and oral culture, we have to construe and add meaning in narratives written by the Britishers who often would grandly boast about their achievements in India. Even if we hear little from the natives at this time period of print technology in Calcutta, the Britishers were extravagant in their rhetoric when it came to describing the need for print in India: "amidst the numerous blessings which have flowed from it [the rule of England], one of the most important is, the introduction of that mighty engine of improvement to which Europe is itself so highly indebted — the Press."[7] An editorial in a newspaper summarizes the presence of the native press in laudatory terms, as if justifying the good of colonial rule:

> The era of improvement and of civilization has already dawned on this country. The Natives possess a Press of their own, and its operations have commenced with that vigour and effect which warrant the most sanguine expectations. Within the last ten years, native works have been printed by Natives themselves, and sold among the Hindoo population with astonishing rapidity. An unprecedented impulse has been communicated to the inhabitants of Bengal, and the avidity for reading has increased beyond all former example. Before this period, the press had been confined to Europeans, and the only works in the native languages were printed at their expense, and circulated gratis. The natives have now taken the work into their own hands, and the commencement is commensurate with the avarice of native editors, and the rich fund of

---

pp. i-liii, p. xxv. In *The Annals*, there is also mention on the importance of preserving old manuscripts: "The preservation and augmentation of the Collection of Eastern Manuscripts, afford the only means of arresting the progressive destruction of Oriental learning. Since the dismemberment of the Muslim, those works have been dispersed over India, and have been exposed to the injuries and hazards of time, accident and neglect. It is worthy of the ambition of this great Empire to employ every effort of its influence in preserving from destruction and decay, these valuable records of Oriental history, Science and Religion." p. 114.

[7] "Art. V. - On the effect of the Native Press in India," *The Friend of India*. Quarterly Series (No. 1): 130-154, pp. 132-133.

wealth enjoyed by the higher class of Hindoos.[8]

As readers situated in the present where print is prolific and an intrinsic element in our lives, we really are unable to comprehend how printed texts would have affected a manuscript culture, and often we are given an interpretation which would have to be partially biased, as it comes from the perspective of the Britishers. The editorial continues in a similar extravagant manner:

> The multiplication of printed works has excited a taste for reading, hitherto unknown in India, which promises to become gradually more extensive and more refined. Compared with preceding years, when manuscripts alone existed, books are now exceedingly common: men of wealth and influence begin already to value themselves on the possession of a library, and on obtaining the earliest intelligence of the operations of the press. Even among the inferior gentry, there are few who do not possess some of the works which the press has created. The country partakes of the same spirit with the metropolis, though in an inferior degree. The encouragement afforded to this incipient plan, has likewise called forth a race of editors.[9]

Within a span of a few decades, the editorial writes, a "body of enlightened natives animated with an unconquerable thirst for knowledge" would emerge. There is a sense that print would allow for the emergence of a new kind of a print-informed native, and large societal changes would enable a realm of print culture to be established, with readers, writers, editors, distributors and so on.

---

[8] Ibid., p. 133.

[9] Ibid., p. 135.

The emergence of early newspaper print in colonial Calcutta.

Oftentimes, the enormous justification as to why there was a need to colonize India was transferred onto the natives who were construed as wanting progress from the west. We can only imagine how the print informed landscape in Calcutta would have changed in the last two decades of the eighteenth century; presses, paper, books, magazines and other print paraphernalia would have arrived as cargo in the ships from England, they would be carted across and stored somewhere and then subsequently bought by printers and booksellers. The central assumption within eighteenth century British print culture, where print technology was seen at the apex of communication forms, was transferred onto the colonies by the East India Company. Such was the realm of print that evolved in Calcutta, in the last two decades of the twentieth century, serving the needs of the empire.

2. READING NEWS IN CALCUTTA, CIRCA 1780 OR SO: WAR, POLITICS AND HABITS OF CONSUMPTION IN THE REALM OF IMPERIAL PRINT.

The initial realm of print culture in Calcutta not only featured Orientalist scholarship and grammar books, but a large percentage of printed material was of a non-literary kind—stationery, handbills, advertisements, catalogues, legal and mercantile blank forms, calendars and almanacs. The print industry, though, was dominated by newspapers; it was "around the production of weekly newspapers that the whole commercial printing-trade in eighteenth century Calcutta was organized."[10] Twenty four weekly and monthly newspapers were published in the last two decades of the eighteenth century. For a publication to be successful, the patronage of the East India Company was essential.[11] Most of the newspapers were unable to continue beyond a few years and yet this did not prevent the publication of new newspapers. An editorial comment in the *Calcutta Chronicle* put it most succinctly:

> The proprietors of the *Calcutta Chronicle*, in consequence of the large amount of the bills now due to them, (many of them, of several years standing), request these Gentlemen indebted to the Office, will have the goodness to direct the payment of their bills, when presented either to themselves or agents. The aggregate amount of the bills, now outstanding is near 60,000 rupees, the bare interest of so large a sum, amounts to a considerable sum monthly, and as the proprietors have suffered much inconvenience and great loss, from so large an amount being outstanding, they beg to give notice that all bills, &. which remain unpaid on the 31st December next, will, on the 1st of January 1793, be put into the hands of an attorney, to recover by a legal course.[12]

---

[10] Shaw, *Printing in Calcutta*, p. 3.

[11] Ibid., p. 26.

[12] *Calcutta Chronicle*. 1 Jan, 1793, vii, 363, 2.

The emergence of early newspaper print in colonial Calcutta.

Before 1800, all the printing presses were run by Europeans, and staffed by natives. According to Hadjee Mustapha, who was writing around 1790: "There are but four Printing Offices at Calcutta, amongst which one only is worked by Europeans, that of Cooper's: the three others, although inspected by an European, are worked by natives, who print in a Printing Office, just as they copy in a Counting House, without understanding the language."[13] Native Brahmins, blacksmiths and Englishmen worked side by side in these printing houses, participating in a technological and intellectual exchange that was revolutionary in most ways. The printing house also became a heterogeneous social space.

In *Printing in Calcutta to 1800*, Graham Shaw documents the number of presses that were in operation till 1800.[14] From 1780 to 1790, there were between three and five presses continually in operation, and from 1791 to 1799, between seven and ten active in each year. The presses were mostly concerned with the printing of newspapers, and the increase reflects the opening of newspaper offices in Calcutta in 1791-2. All the newspapers were meant to be read by the British residents, aiding in and enabling the formation of imperial identity. When we try to recover the nature of readership from these early printed texts, we have to look at the historical context within which these newspapers were written. The diasporic community was the targeted readers, and the locale of readership meant that these texts were read by a select audience. For the small fledgling community of British traders and administrators, print was a medium of communication with the metropoles, and between themselves. In the first issue of *The World*, on 15 October 1791, William Duane wrote with great aplomb that the "civilized world affords no similar instance in the rise and culture of the arts, and to such perfection as Calcutta this day affords – the mechanical arts, which depend on the luxuries of society, and the tangibility of fashion, are arrived to the summit of perfection."[15] And he continued in a laudatory note that "in no respects can she [Calcutta] appear so eminently

---

[13] Quoted in Shaw, *Printing in Calcutta*, p. 3.

[14] Graham Shaw, *Printing in Calcutta to 1800* (London: The Bibliographical Society, 1981).

[15] Quoted in Shaw, *Printing in Calcutta*, p. 4.

so, as in her publications … If in Europe, the number of publications give the grounds to ratiocinate the learning and refinement of particular cities, we may place Calcutta in rank above Vienna, Copenhagen, Petersburg, Madrid, Venice, Turin, Naples, or even Rome."[16] Print culture played an important role in the lives of this expatriate community of diasporic residents who carried with them the culture of print from eighteenth century England, that was still in a state of transit as it shifted away from oral and manuscript cultures.

If we go in search of the origins of the newspaper in Calcutta, we go all the way to eighteenth-century England, if not earlier, and this is a fascinating thought: that a printed text that is so intrinsic to our everyday lives has its origins in a foreign country, and was carried across and established by the English in the city for their own specific needs. As printing presses and editors were imported from England, it is not surprising that the very format, structure and content of newspapers in Calcutta are replicas of those of English newspapers. Hence, when discussing the evolution of newspapers in Calcutta, we have to keep in mind the nature of the newspaper in England, and how newsbooks of the seventeenth century became printed newspapers by the end of the century. Newspapers that were printed in Calcutta in the last two decades of the eighteenth century performed a very important function in the very fabric of the existence of the settler community – allowing those in the metropole in Calcutta to consider themselves as connected to the daily activities of the center. A print induced sub public emerged, replete with discourses of empire and colonization. A sense of diasporic, imperial citizenship was formed as a result of the consumption of newspapers.

---

[16] Ibid., p. 4.

The emergence of early newspaper print in colonial Calcutta.

I: Habits of consumption. Reading advertisements.

A large section of the newspapers that were printed in Calcutta were filled with advertisements, because without advertisements in newspapers, goods that were brought from Europe could not be publicly made known to the residents. The men could not do without claret and cheeses, and the women could not survive without stockings and hats. The relationship between traders, the European residents of Bengal and print culture is an intrinsic one, and goods that were imported and advertised through print had to be sold to the English residents. This was the function of print advertisements, and a public notice set up in 1768 in a commercial area of Calcutta, by one William Bolts, addressed to the "Public" draws -attention to the importance of print technology: "Mr Bolts takes this method of informing the public that the want of a printing press in this city being of great disadvantage in business, and making it extremely difficult to communicate such intelligence to the community as is of the utmost importance to every British subject."[17] And even if the newspaper had little circulation and subscription, advertisements made it economically possible for the newspaper to be printed. Newspaper publishers were fully cognizant of this fact and took advantage of the consumer fetishism displayed by the British. All newspapers had an alternative title; the full title of the *Bengal Gazette* was the *Bengal Gazette or Calcutta General Advertiser*; likewise the *India Gazette* was also subtitled *India Gazette, or Calcutta Public Advertiser*. These social habits of consumption made it possible for the rich and the educated English to live in India. Those who lived in Calcutta had similar habits of consumption and they were bound to the metropole of London through these social habits.

Advertisements that were plenty in the early newspapers in Calcutta reflect the consumerist lifestyle of the British residents who lived there towards the end of the eighteenth century. These habits of consumption were definitive of the identity of the Britishers. Advertisements would appear that would proclaim the sale of goods from ships that had arrived

---

[17] Quoted in Thankappan Nair, *A History of the Calcutta Press* (Calcutta: KLM Firma, 1987), p. 1.

from England (fig. 2):[18] claret, red port, brandy, Jamaica rum and other varieties of alcohol, ham, pickled tongues, cheeses, salad oils, olives, raisins, currants, almonds, milk chocolate, confectionary, looking glasses, glassware, floor cloths, ladies and gentlemen's silk and cotton stockings, hats, cloth and cashmere, waistcoats shapes, boat cloaks, leather breeches and gloves, silk and cotton gloves, Irish linen, French cambric, Manchester goods of different sorts, books, stationary, perfumery, rifle guns, spare locks, gun powder and shot. Another advertisement (fig. 3) stated that goods that were imported from Dublin were to be sold by auction: Four hawsers, sixteen coils of small rope, a quantity of patent blocks, a sextant, a case of artillery, mathematical instruments, a theodolite in a mahogany case, twenty kegs of paints, one hundred pounds of chocolates, fifty pots of spruce, two sets of china ware, fifty pieces of white handkerchiefs, two bureaus, a harpsichord, some buggy and phaeton harness, a roasting jack, seventeen cases of Holland's gin, a pipe of Madeira, a quantity of Chittagong Red Wood. Considering the extent to which advertisements were featured in the newspapers, it is not a farfetched idea to state that British-ness in the colonies was defined through the capacity to consume commodities and objects.

---

[18] *Calcutta Chronicle*, 3 April (1792): 3.

The emergence of early newspaper print in colonial Calcutta.

Figure 2: Habits of consumption; advertisements for goods.

Figure 3: Habits of consumption; more advertisements for goods.

The emergence of early newspaper print in colonial Calcutta.

II: Newspapers and British Imperial Identity: War, politics of the state and public affairs.

The newspaper print culture in eighteenth century England was able to bind the people within the frame of imperial citizenry, and even those in the provinces identified with the political processes of the state, nation and empire. Most newspapers carried news of war, trade and imperial expansion, shaping the readers notions of the nation and the empire, and British national identity rested on incorporating the colonies within the national imaginary. The print-induced English sub-public was replete with images of the colonies where the British Empire spread across continents. All printed books in native languages in the realm of early print which targeted British readers implied that the natives were also part of the Empire. For example, a review of Nathaniel Halhed's *Grammar of the Bengal Language* in the *English Review* in 1783 makes an easy equation between the study of Indian languages and their use in maintaining the British empire in India; "… we shall confine our observations to strictures on the history and usefulness of a language of very high antiquity, spoken by millions of industrious British subjects."[19] For Halhed, the British Empire embraced the newly formed native subjects into becoming "industrious British subjects."

A large section of the newspapers that were printed in Bengal chronicled news from Europe that was six months old. The Empire was formed in the imagination of the English readers through these narratives. For example, in the *Calcutta Chronicle*, on May 29, 1792,[20] there are summaries from other British newspapers of the previous year: the *Gazetteer*, Dec. 15, the *General Evening Post* Dec. 3, and the *Morning Post*. Dec. 15 (fig.4). The British readers in Bengal were kept informed of the wars that

---

[19] "Review of Halhed's *Grammar of the Bengal Language*," *The English Review, or, An Abstract of English and Foreign Literature* 1(1783): 5-14.

[20] *Calcutta Chronicle,* 29 May (1792): 1.

Tapati Bharadwaj

Figure 4: Summaries from six month old British newspapers.

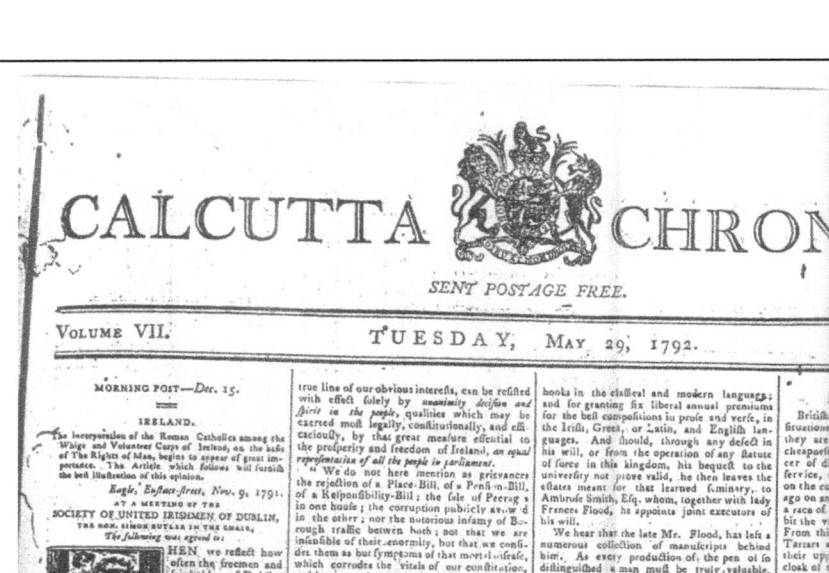

The emergence of early newspaper print in colonial Calcutta.

were waged across the globe and of news from the different colonies. Extracts from state papers also featured in the newspapers; an instance is evident in the news of the "Secret Convention entered on the 5th of August, 1795, at Berlin, between His Majesty the King of Prussia and the French Republic" that was published in the *Calcutta Gazette* on February 6, 1800 (fig.5). Foreign news and their analyses were prominent; the *Supplement to the Calcutta Gazette*, on June 9, 1796 (fig.6) chronicled the wars on the Continent, alongside "Remarks on the Apparent Circumstances of the War, in the fourth week of October, 1795." As the news was old, it performed a function akin to a pseudo-historical narrative, reminding the readers of their role in global affairs and giving meaning and coherence to their identities as imperialists—those residing in the colonies were reminded that they were part of the Empire. In some ways, the newspapers were akin to novels but, as Anderson says, of an "ephemeral," nature.[21] The English were portrayed as winners in all the accounts of war. These were akin to the periodicals in eighteenth century England where colonial events were narrated in such a manner so as to cast the British as superior and morally right, thus cultivating a sense of legitimacy in the processes of Empire formation.

---

[21] Benedict Anderson, *Imagined Communities: reflections on the origin and spread of nationalism* (New York: Verso, 1991).

Figure 5: Extracts from State Papers.

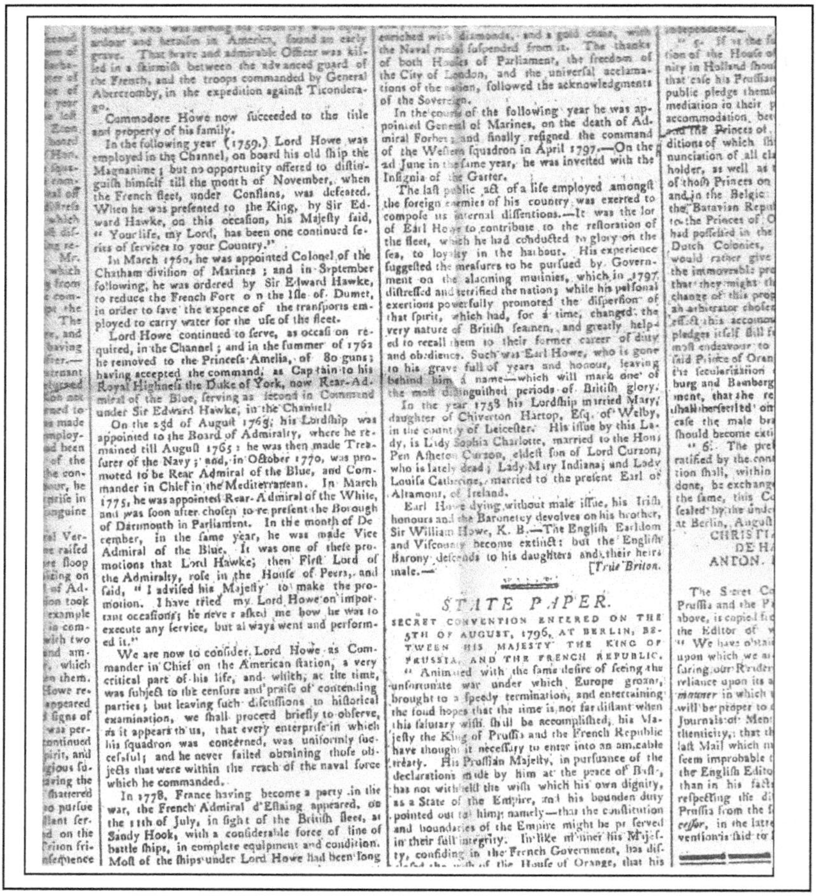

[...] brother, who was serving his country with equal ardour and heroism in America, found an early grave. That brave and admirable Officer was killed in a skirmish between the advanced guard of the French, and the troops commanded by General Abercromby, in the expedition against Ticonderago.

Commodore Howe now succeeded to the title and property of his family.

In the following year (1759.) Lord Howe was employed in the Channel, on board his old ship the Magnanime; but no opportunity offered to distinguish himself till the month of November, when the French fleet, under Conflans, was defeated. When he was presented to the King, by Sir Edward Hawke, on this occasion, his Majesty said, "Your life, my Lord, has been one continued series of services to your Country."

In March 1760, he was appointed Colonel of the Chatham division of Marines; and in September following, he was ordered by Sir Edward Hawke, to reduce the French Fort on the Isle of Dumet, in order to save the expence of the transports employed to carry water for the use of the fleet.

Lord Howe continued to serve, as occasion required, in the Channel; and in the summer of 1762 he removed to the Princess Amelia, of 80 guns; having accepted the command, as Captain to his Royal Highness the Duke of York, now Rear-Admiral of the Blue, serving as second in Command under Sir Edward Hawke, in the Channel.

On the 23d of August 1763, his Lordship was appointed to the Board of Admiralty, where he remained till August 1765: he was then made Treasurer of the Navy; and, in October 1770, was promoted to be Rear Admiral of the Blue, and Commander in Chief in the Mediterranean. In March 1775, he was appointed Rear-Admiral of the White, and was soon after chosen to represent the Borough of Dartmouth in Parliament. In the month of December, in the same year, he was made Vice Admiral of the Blue. It was one of these promotions that Lord Hawke, then First Lord of the Admiralty, rose in the House of Peers, and said, "I advised his Majesty to make the promotion. I have tried my Lord Howe on important occasions; he never asked me how he was to execute any service, but always went and performed it."

We are now to consider Lord Howe as Commander in Chief on the American station, a very critical part of his life, and which, at the time, was subject to the censure and praise of contending parties; but leaving such discussions to historical examination, we shall proceed briefly to observe, as it appears to us, that every enterprise in which his squadron was concerned, was uniformly successful; and he never failed obtaining those objects that were within the reach of the naval force which he commanded.

In 1778, France having become a party in the war, the French Admiral d'Estaing appeared, on the 11th of July, in sight of the British fleet, at Sandy Hook, with a considerable force of line of battle ships, in complete equipment and condition. Most of the ships under Lord Howe had been long [...]

[...] enriched with diamonds, and a gold chain, with the Naval medal suspended from it. The thanks of both Houses of Parliament, the freedom of the City of London, and the universal acclamations of the nation, followed the acknowledgments of the Sovereign.

In the course of the following year he was appointed General of Marines, on the death of Admiral Forbes; and finally resigned the command of the Western squadron in April 1797.—On the 2d June in the same year, he was invested with the Insignia of the Garter.

The last public act of a life employed amongst the foreign enemies of his country was exerted to compose its internal dissentions.—It was the lot of Earl Howe to contribute to the restoration of the fleet, which he had conducted to glory on the sea, to loyalty in the harbour. His experience suggested the measures to be pursued by Government on the alarming mutinies, which in 1797 distressed and terrified the nation; while his personal exertions powerfully promoted the dispersion of that spirit, which had, for a time, changed the very nature of British seamen, and greatly helped to recall them to their former career of duty and obedience. Such was Earl Howe, who is gone to his grave full of years and honour, leaving behind him a name—which will mark one of the most distinguished periods of British glory.

In the year 1758 his Lordship married Mary, daughter of Chiverton Hartop, Esq. of Welby, in the county of Leicester. His issue by this Lady, is Lady Sophia Charlotte, married to the Hon. Pen Assheton Curzon, eldest son of Lord Curzon, who is lately dead; Lady Mary Indiana; and Lady Louisa Catherine, married to the present Earl of Altamont, of Ireland.

Earl Howe dying without male issue, his Irish honours and the Baronetcy devolves on his brother, Sir William Howe, K. B.—The English Earldom and Viscounty become extinct: but the English Barony descends to his daughters and their heirs male.— [True Briton.

STATE PAPER.

SECRET CONVENTION ENTERED ON THE 5TH OF AUGUST, 1796, AT BERLIN, BETWEEN HIS MAJESTY THE KING OF PRUSSIA, AND THE FRENCH REPUBLIC.

"Animated with the same desire of seeing the unfortunate war under which Europe groans, brought to a speedy termination, and entertaining the fond hopes that the time is not far distant when this salutary wish shall be accomplished, his Majesty the King of Prussia and the French Republic have thought it necessary to enter into an amicable treaty. His Prussian Majesty, in pursuance of the declarations made by him at the peace of Basle, has not withheld the wish which his own dignity, as a State of the Empire, and his bounden duty pointed out to him; namely—that the constitution and boundaries of the Empire might be preserved in their full integrity. In like manner his Majesty, confiding in the French Government, has dis- [...] of the House of Orange, that his [...]

The emergence of early newspaper print in colonial Calcutta.

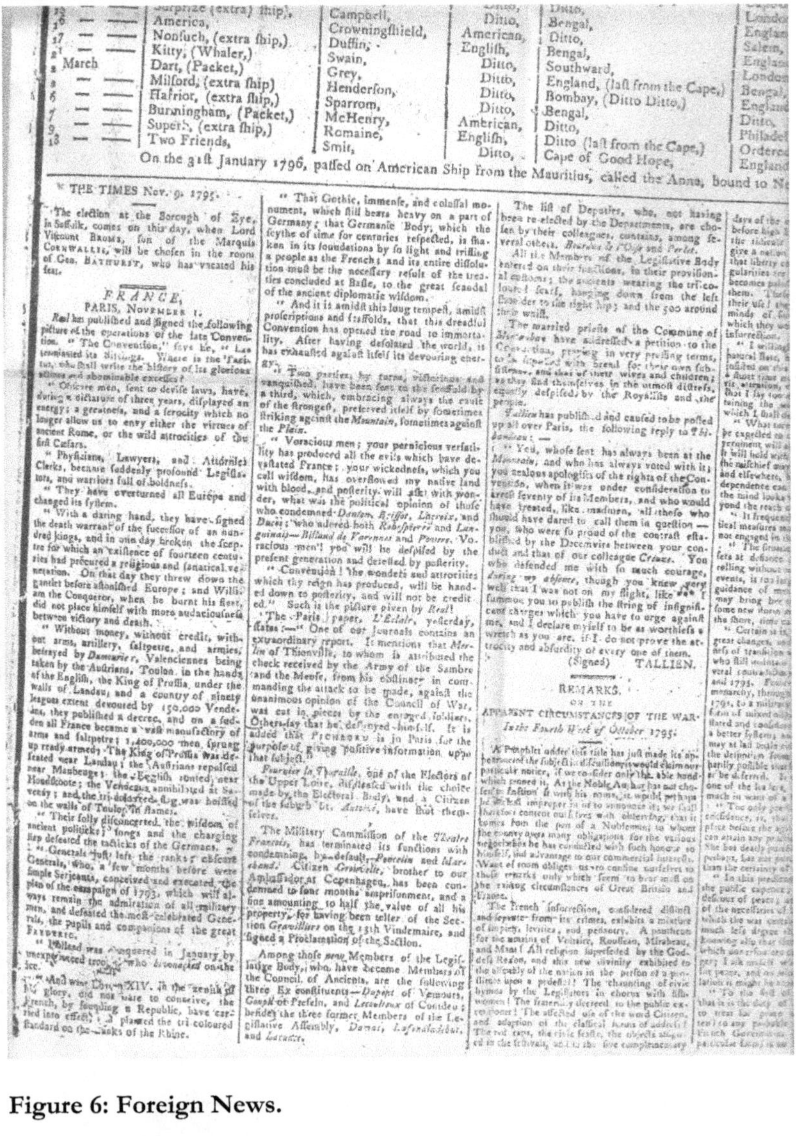

[illegible]	— —	Surprize (extra) ſhip,		Ditto,	Ditto,	
16	— —	America,	Campbell,	Ditto,	Bengal,	London
17	— —	Nonſuch, (extra ſhip,)	Crowningſhield,	American,	Ditto,	England
21	— —	Kitty, (Whaler,)	Duffin,	Engliſh,	Bengal,	Salem,
2	March	Dart, (Packet,)	Swain,	Ditto,	Southward,	England
2	— —	Milford, (extra ſhip)	Grey,	Ditto,	England, (laſt from the Cape,)	London
6	— —	Hafrior, (extra ſhip,)	Henderſon,	Ditto,	Bombay, (Ditto Ditto,)	Bengal,
7	— —	Burnningham, (Packet,)	Sparrom,	Ditto,	Bengal,	England
9	— —	Superb, (extra ſhip,)	McHenry,	American,	Ditto,	Ditto,
13	— —	Two Friends,	Romaine,	Engliſh,	Ditto (laſt from the Cape,)	Philadel
			Smit,	Ditto,	Cape of Good Hope,	Ordered
						England

On the 31ſt January 1796, paſſed an American Ship from the Mauritius, called the Anna, bound to N[illegible]

THE TIMES Nov. 9. 1795.

The election at the Borough of Eye, in Suffolk, comes on this day, when Lord Viſcount Brome, ſon of the Marquis Cornwallis, will be choſen in the room of Gen. Bathurst, who has vacated his ſeat.

FRANCE,

PARIS, November 1.

Real has publiſhed and ſigned the following picture of the operations of the late Convention. "The Convention," ſays he, "has terminated its Sittings. Where is the Tacitus, who ſhall write the hiſtory of its glorious actions and abominable exceſſes?

"Obſcure men, ſent to deviſe laws, have, during a dictature of three years, diſplayed an energy; a greatneſs, and a ferocity which no longer allow us to envy either the virtues of ancient Rome, or the wild atrocities of the firſt Cæſars.

"Phyſicians, Lawyers, and Attornies Clerks, became ſuddenly profound Legiſlators, and warriors full of boldneſs.

"They have overturned all Europe and changed its ſyſtem.

"With a daring hand, they have ſigned the death warrant of the ſucceſſor of an hundred kings, and in one day broken the ſceptre for which an exiſtence of fourteen centuries had procured a religious and fanatical veneration. On that day they threw down the gantlet before aſtoniſhed Europe; and William the Conqueror, when he burnt his fleet, did not place himſelf with more audaciouſneſs between victory and death.

"Without money, without credit, without arms, artillery, ſaltpetre, and armies; betrayed by *Dumourier*, Valenciennes being taken by the Auſtrians, Toulon in the hands of the Engliſh, the King of Pruſſia under the walls of Landau, and a country of ninety leagues extent devoured by 150,000 Vendeans, they publiſhed a decree, and on a ſudden all France became a vaſt manufactory of arms and ſaltpetre; 1,400,000 men ſprung up ready armed. The King of Pruſſia was defeated near Landau; the Auſtrians repulſed near Maubeuge; the Engliſh routed near Hondſchoote; the Vendeans annihilated at Savenay; and the tri-coloured flag was hoiſted on the walls of Toulon in flames.

"Their folly diſconcerted the wiſdom of ancient politicks; ſongs and the charging ſtep defeated the tacticks of the Germans.

"Generals juſt left the ranks; obſcure Generals, who, a few months before were ſimple Serjeants, conceived and executed the plan of the campaign of 1793, which will always remain the admiration of all military men, and defeated the moſt celebrated Generals, the pupils and companions of the great Frederic.

"Holland was conquered in January by unexperienced troops, who *bivouacked* on the ice.

"And what Louis XIV. in the zenith of his glory, did not dare to conceive, the French, by founding a Republic, have carried into effect, and planted the tri-coloured ſtandard on the banks of the Rhine.

"That Gothic, immenſe, and coloſſal monument, which ſtill bears heavy on a part of Germany; that Germanic Body, which the ſcythe of time for centuries reſpected, is ſhaken in its foundations by ſo light and trifling a people as the French; and its entire diſſolution muſt be the neceſſary reſult of the treaties concluded at Baſle, to the great ſcandal of the ancient diplomatic wiſdom.

"And it is amidſt this long tempeſt, amidſt proſcriptions and ſcaffolds, that this dreadful Convention has opened the road to immortality. After having deſolated the world, it has exhauſted againſt itſelf its devouring energy.

"Two parties, by turns, victorious and vanquiſhed, have been ſent to the ſcaffold by a third, which, embracing always the cauſe of the ſtrongeſt, preſerved itſelf by ſometimes ſtriking againſt the *Mountain*, ſometimes againſt the *Plain*.

"Voracious men; your pernicious verſatility has produced all the evils which have devaſtated France; your wickedneſs, which you call wiſdom, has overflowed my native land with blood, and poſterity will aſk with wonder, what was the political opinion of thoſe who condemned *Danton*, *Briſſot*, *Lacroix*, and *Ducos*; who adored both *Robeſpierre* and *Lanjuinais*—*Billaud de Varennes* and *Pouvre*. Voracious men! you will be deſpiſed by the preſent generation and deteſted by poſterity.

"Convention! the wonders and atrocities which thy reign has produced, will be handed down to poſterity, and will not be credited." Such is the picture given by *Real*!

The Paris paper, *L'Eclair*, yeſterday, ſtates:—" One of our Journals contains an extraordinary report. It mentions that *Merlin* of Thionville, to whom is attributed the check received by the Army of the Sambre and the Meuſe, from his obſtinacy in commanding the attack to be made, againſt the unanimous opinion of the Council of War, was cut in pieces by the enraged ſoldiers. Others ſay that he deſtroyed himſelf. It is added that Pichegru is in Paris for the purpoſe of giving poſitive information upon that ſubject."

Fournier la Thoraille, one of the Electors of the Upper Loire, diſpleaſed with the choice made by the Electoral Body, and a Citizen of the ſuburb St. *Antoine*, have ſhot themſelves.

The Military Commiſſion of the *Theatre Francois*, has terminated its functions with condemning, by default, *Porcelin* and *Marchand*. Citizen *Grouvelle*, brother to our Ambaſſador at Copenhagen, has been condemned to four months impriſonment, and a fine amounting to half the value of all his property, for having been teller of the Section *Gravilliers* on the 13th Vindemaire, and ſigned a Proclamation of the Section.

Among thoſe new Members of the Legiſlative Body, who have become Members of the Council of Ancients, are the following three Ex conſtituents—*Dupont* of Nemours, *Goupil* of Prefeln, and *Lecoulteux* of Conteleu; beſides the three former Members of the Legiſlative Aſſembly, *Dumas*, *Lafondladebat*, and *Lacuee*.

The liſt of Deputies, who, not having been re-elected by the Departments, are choſen by their colleagues, contains, among ſeveral others, *Bourdon de l'Oiſe* and *Perlet*.

All the Members of the Legiſlative Body entered on their functions, in their proviſional cuſtoms; the ancients wearing the tri-coloured ſcarf, hanging down from the left ſhoulder to the right hip; and the 500 around their waiſt.

The married prieſts of the Commune of [illegible] have addreſſed a petition to the Convention, praying in very preſſing terms, to be ſupplied with bread for their own ſubſiſtence, and that of their wives and children; as they find themſelves in the utmoſt diſtreſs, equally deſpiſed by the Royaliſts and the people.

Tallien has publiſhed and cauſed to be poſted up all over Paris, the following reply to *Thibaudeau*:—

"You, whoſe ſeat has always been at the *Mountain*, and who has always voted with it; you zealous apologiſts of the rights of the Convention, when it was under conſideration to arreſt ſeventy of its Members, and who would have treated, like madmen, all thoſe who ſhould have dared to call them in queſtion—you, who were ſo proud of the contraſt eſtabliſhed by the Decemvirs between your conduct and that of our colleague *Crance*. You who defended me with ſo much courage, *during my abſence*, though you knew very well that I was not on my flight, like *** I ſummon you to publiſh the ſtring of inſignificant charges which you have to urge againſt me, and I declare myſelf to be as worthleſs a wretch as you are, if I do not prove the atrocity and abſurdity of every one of them.

(Signed) TALLIEN.

REMARKS,

ON THE

APPARENT CIRCUMSTANCES OF THE WAR.

In the Fourth Week of October 1795.

A Pamphlet under this title has juſt made its appearance, the ſubject [illegible] would claim our particular notice, if we conſider only the able hand which penned it. As the Noble Author has not choſen to faſhion it with his name, it would perhaps be deemed improper in us to announce it; we ſhall therefore content ourſelves with obſerving, that it comes from the pen of a Nobleman, to whom the country owes many obligations for the various negociations he has conducted with ſuch honour to himſelf, and advantage to our commercial intereſts. Want of room obliges us to confine ourſelves to thoſe remarks only which ſeem to bear moſt on the exiſting circumſtances of Great Britain and France.

The French Inſurrection, conſidered diſtinct and ſeparate from its crimes, exhibits a mixture of impiety, levities, and pedantry. A pantheon for the remains of Voltaire, Rouſſeau, Mirabeau, and Marat! All religion ſuperſeded by the Goddeſs Reaſon, and this new divinity exhibited to the aſſembly of the nation in the perſon of a proſtitute upon a pedeſtal! The chaunting of civic hymns by the Legiſlators in chorus with fiſhwomen! The fraternity decreed to the public executioner! The affected uſe of the word Citizen, and adoption of the claſſical forms of addreſs! The red caps, the civic feaſts, the objects [illegible] ed in the feſtivals, and [illegible] the five complimentary [illegible]

Figure 6: Foreign News.

The eighteenth century newspaper and journal was made out of different literary forms, and was a hybrid of sorts, a mixture of fiction and news. The periodical of the eighteenth century was an undefined, shapeless pastiche made out of different genres from different writers. Journalistic essays and poetry were included. Barbara Benedict[22] writes that it was a mélange of "fact, fiction, literature and gossip" whereby literature was indistinguishable from news.[23] Past events when retold in the newspapers often read like a story. For the reader, situated in Calcutta, a notion of the Empire was created through the narratives in the newspapers that described victories that were fought, both local and global, using dominant tropes and motifs of war and exoticity. The newspapers featured recent news that narrated wars that had happened within India, and concerned the British; events that did not involve the British were not reported. An apt instance is the official correspondence between Cornwallis, a governor General of India (1786-1793) and the British government. Cornwallis was involved in a major war that the British fought against one of the ruling kings of South India, Tipu Sultan. A letter that Cornwallis had written to the secretary of State on October 5, 1791, was printed in an Indian newspaper about six months later (fig. 7). The war was described as a major victory that clinched south India. He wrote:

> …. [various branches of business] obliged me to confine myself to a very concise statement of the principal occurrences, in my letter to the East India Company; but, by the means of that letter, and the copies of my correspondence with the residents at the Courts of Hyderabad and Poonah, and of my late letters to the Governor of Fort St. George, which will no doubt be transmitted to you from the India-House, you will have it in your power to convey to His Majesty a general knowledge of the present situation of our affairs in this

---

[22] Barbara Benedict, *Readers, Writers, Reviewers and the Professionalization of Literature* (Cambridge: Cambridge University Press, 2006).

[23] Anderson, *Imagined Communities,* p. 10.

The emergence of early newspaper print in colonial Calcutta.

Figure 7: Letter written by Cornwallis to the Secretary of State about the Mysore wars.

> country; and you will have the satisfaction to observe, not only that our success has already been considerable, ...
> Our success at Bangalore has tended to establish, in the general opinion of the natives, the superiority of the British arms; and it has, in particular, made an impression upon the minds of our allies ...[24]

The official treaty that was signed between Cornwallis and Tipu Sultan was published in the newspapers, allowing the English readers to actively participate in the political processes that were in operation (fig. 8). The victory was portrayed as the final defeat of India. The sons of the defeated king were taken as captive hostages, and this capture was described as the possession of the wealth of India. Their public entry was described in extravagant terms (fig. 9):

> [The] dresses of the Princes were splendid – they were covered almost with a profusion of jewels. Several valuable strings of pearls were hung round their necks; to which there were appendant a large buckle of diamonds, with a colored stone of immense fire in the center. Their turbans were decorated likewise with rare jewels, set with great taste. ... The attendance of the princes may be said to be not only numerous but splendid of its kind.[25]

News of the war against Tipu Sultan was a regular feature in 1792. The news from the *Madras Courier*, from March 15, 1792, was published in the *Calcutta Chronicle*, on April 10th, 1792: "[the newspaper] is laying before the public the following detail of [war] which comes from good authority." Newspapers made comprehensive events that were taking place and involved the Britishers, making clear to them the power of the British army.

---

[24] *Calcutta Chronicle*. 24 April (1792): 1-2.

[25] *Calcutta Chronicle*. 26 June (1792): 2.

The emergence of early newspaper print in colonial Calcutta.

Figure 8: Official treaty signed between Cornwallis and Tipu Sultan.

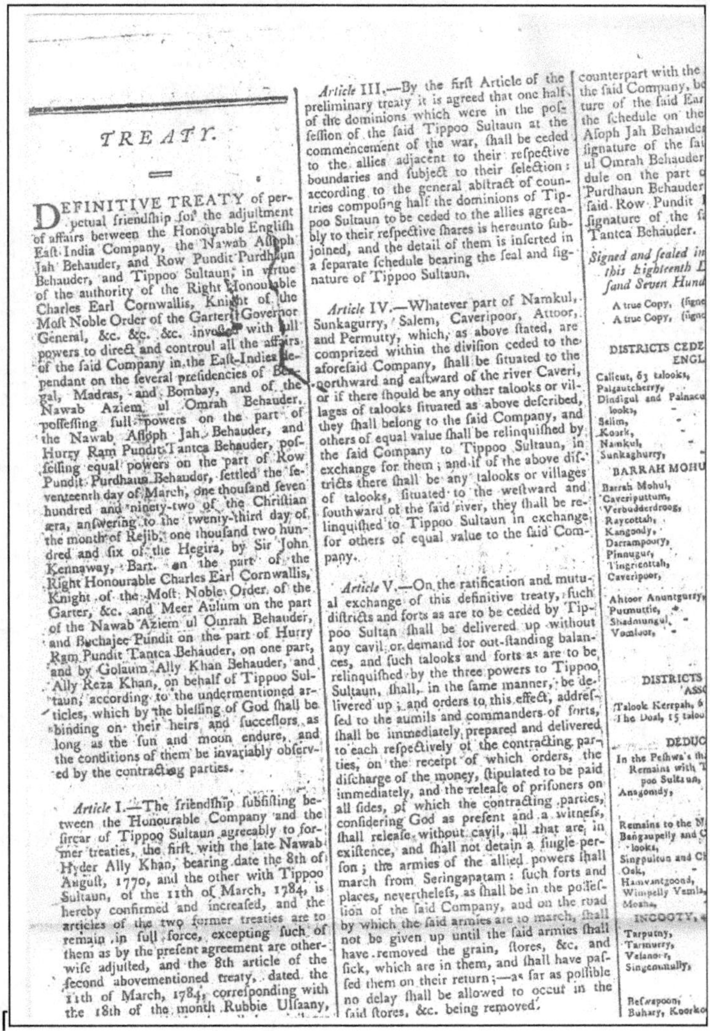

TREATY.

DEFINITIVE TREATY of perpetual friendship for the adjustment of affairs between the Honourable English East-India Company, the Nawab Affoph Jah Behauder, and Row Pundit Purdhaun Behauder, and Tippoo Sultaun; in virtue of the authority of the Right Honourable Charles Earl Cornwallis, Knight of the Most Noble Order of the Garter, Governor General, &c. &c. &c. invested with all powers to direct and controul all the affairs of the said Company in the East-Indies dependant on the several presidencies of Bengal, Madras, and Bombay, and of the Nawab Aziem ul Omrah Behauder, possessing full powers on the part of the Nawab Affoph Jah Behauder, and Hurry Ram Pundit Tantea Behauder, possessing equal powers on the part of Row Pundit Purdhaun Behauder, settled the seventeenth day of March, one thousand seven hundred and ninety-two of the Christian era, answering to the twenty-third day of the month of Rejib, one thousand two hundred and six of the Hegira, by Sir John Kennaway, Bart. on the part of the Right Honourable Charles Earl Cornwallis, Knight of the Most Noble Order of the Garter, &c. and Meer Aulum on the part of the Nawab Aziem ul Omrah Behauder, and Buchajee Pundit on the part of Hurry Ram Pundit Tantca Behauder, on one part, and by Golaum Ally Khan Behauder, and Ally Reza Khan, on behalf of Tippoo Sultaun, according to the undermentioned articles, which by the blessing of God shall be binding on their heirs, and successors, as long as the sun and moon endure, and the conditions of them be invariably observed by the contracting parties.

Article I.—The friendship subsisting between the Honourable Company and the sircar of Tippoo Sultaun agreeable to former treaties, the first with the late Nawab Hyder Ally Khan, bearing date the 8th of August, 1770, and the other with Tippoo Sultaun, of the 11th of March, 1784, is hereby confirmed and increased, and the articles of the two former treaties are to remain in full force, excepting such of them as by the present agreement are otherwise adjusted, and the 8th article of the second abovementioned treaty, dated the 11th of March, 1784, corresponding with the 18th of the month Rubbie Ussaany,

Article III.—By the first Article of the preliminary treaty it is agreed that one half of the dominions which were in the possession of the said Tippoo Sultaun at the commencement of the war, shall be ceded to the allies adjacent to their respective boundaries and subject to their selection: according to the general abstract of countries composing half the dominions of Tippoo Sultaun to be ceded to the allies agreeably to their respective shares is hereunto subjoined, and the detail of them is inserted in a separate schedule bearing the seal and signature of Tippoo Sultaun.

Article IV.—Whatever part of Namkul, Sunkagurry, Salem, Caveripoor, Attoor, and Permutty, which, as above stated, are comprized within the division ceded to the aforesaid Company, shall be situated to the northward and eastward of the river Caveri, or if there should be any other talooks or villages of talooks situated as above described, they shall belong to the said Company, and others of equal value shall be relinquished by the said Company to Tippoo Sultaun, in exchange for them; and if of the above districts there shall be any talooks or villages of talooks, situated to the westward and southward of the said river, they shall be relinquished to Tippoo Sultaun in exchange for others of equal value to the said Company.

Article V.—On the ratification and mutual exchange of this definitive treaty, such districts and forts as are to be ceded by Tippoo Sultan shall be delivered up without any cavil or demand for out-standing balances, and such talooks and forts as are to be, relinquished by the three powers to Tippoo Sultaun, shall, in the same manner, be delivered up; and orders to this effect, addressed to the sumils and commanders of forts, shall be immediately prepared and delivered to each respectively of the contracting parties, on the receipt of which orders, the discharge of the money, stipulated to be paid immediately, and the release of prisoners on all sides, of which the contracting parties, considering God as present and a witness, shall release without cavil, all that are, in existence, and shall not detain a single person; the armies of the allied powers shall march from Seringapatam: such forts and places, nevertheless, as shall be in the possession of the said Company, and on the road by which the said armies are to march, shall not be given up until the said armies shall have removed the grain, stores, &c, and sick, which are in them, and shall have passed them on their return;—as far as possible no delay shall be allowed to occur in the said stores, &c. being removed.

counterpart with the said Company, bear the of the said Ear the schedule on the Afoph Jah Behauder signature of the said ul Omrah Behauder dule on the part of Purdhaun Behauder said Row Pundit Tantca Behauder.

Signed and sealed in this eighteenth D *and Seven Hund*

A true Copy, (signe
A true Copy, (signe

DISTRICTS CEDE
ENGL
Calicut, 63 talooks,
Palgautcherry,
Dindigul and Palnacu looks,
Selim,
Koork,
Namkul,
Sunkaghurry,

BARRAH MOHU
Barrah Mohul,
Caveriputtum,
Verbudderdroog,
Raycottah,
Darrampoory,
Pinnugur,
Tingrentalah,
Caveripoor,

Attoor Anantgurry,
Pucmuttie,
Shadmungul,
Vanloor,

DISTRICTS
ASSI
Talook Kerrpah, 6
The Deal, 15 talool

DEDUC
In the Peshwa's th
Remains with T
poo Sultaun,
Anagondy,

Remains to the N
Bangaupelly and C looks,
Sirpuikon and Cl
Oosk,
Hanvantgoond,
Wimpelly Vamla
Moshu,

INCOOTY,
Tarputny,
Tarmurry,
Velanar,
Singonnnally,

Beferapoon,
Buhary, Koorko

Figure 9: Public entry of the captive princes.

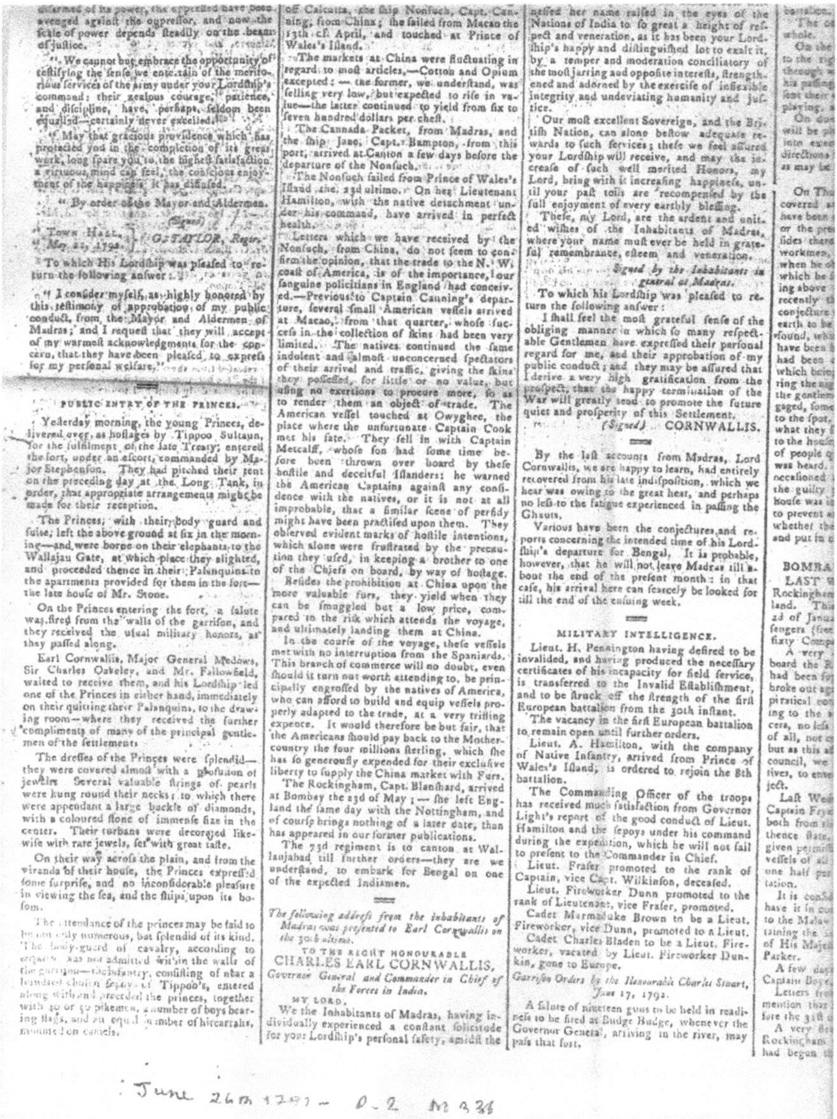

The emergence of early newspaper print in colonial Calcutta.

In 1792, when peace was declared, there was an article in the *Calcutta Chronicle*, with details of the war, and the subsequent treaty that was signed: "The late Peace with Tippu is undoubtedly as advantageous as honorable to the British Government; but it will derive greater glory when contrasted with the Peace of 1784, when we accepted rather than dictated; it serves to show how much our power and superiority has increased since that period, as it has enabled us to prescribe and insist upon a compliance with our own terms, at the walls of our enemy's capital."[26] The British were portrayed as legitimate rulers of India, and the Indians as the enemy. As Ian Atherton[27] writes on the role of history and newspapers:

> It was a seventeenth century commonplace that history could teach useful lessons. ... Gentlemen were adviced to study history for delight and profit. Civil or political history was considered to be none other than an accurate report of past and present facts and events. Reading contemporary history – the news – could, therefore, be as profitable as reading ancient history.[28]

The narrative of history in the newspapers represented India in need of being ruled by the British, and this was intrinsic to establishing a British identity in the colonies, enabling a diasporic notion of imperial citizenship. Even if there was dissent among the British, since escape to the colonies was particularly attractive to those with non-standard beliefs, including Dissenters, they all would have participated in agreeing that India needed to be ruled. Those in the colonies retained many of the characteristics of being a member of the ruling class.

---

[26] *Calcutta Chronicle,* 24 April (1792).

[27] Ian Atherton, "The Itch grown a Disease: Manuscript Transmission of news in the Seventeenth century" in Joan Raymond (ed.), *News, Newspaper and Society in Early Modern Britain* (London: Frank Cass, 1999), pp. 39-65.

[28] Ibid., pp. 45-46.

II: Multilingual Texts.

Between 1780 and 1800, many newspapers in Calcutta printed news in multiple languages side by side on the same sheet of paper (fig.10). This was a moment in the history of newspapers in England and in India that had not happened before and was not replicated subsequently. Any reader of these beautiful multilingual sheets of paper would question as to why such newspapers went out of fashion within a few decades after they were printed. Not only had the new technology of print culture entered India with the Britishers but also, this technology, in the process of establishing itself within a colonial situation, underwent changes on how it was conceptualized. Colonization determined the nature of print culture which is why multilingual newspapers emerged in Calcutta and for a few moments in the history of print culture and of newspapers, there were such heteroglossic texts. The sheer new-ness of the visual text was and is mind-boggling in all respects – specially if we see how radical it was conceptually.

Is it possible that such a multilingual text could only happen in south Asia where a multilingual society exists. In some ways, and unwittingly so, the Britishers captured an aspect of Indian society within these printed texts and the sheer spirit of invention marks this heteroglossic text. The possibilities of what could have been if newspapers had continued to be multilingual are not explored for the emergence of such texts marks an epistemic shift, thus answering an unasked but obviously implied question: what happens when a technology that has its origins in a different social space enters a new geographical locale and how does it change? The heteroglossic nature of Indian society was reflected in how these newspapers were formed; moreover, in some ways, the Britishers were attempting to portray and capture Indian society in these newspapers.

The emergence of early newspaper print in colonial Calcutta.

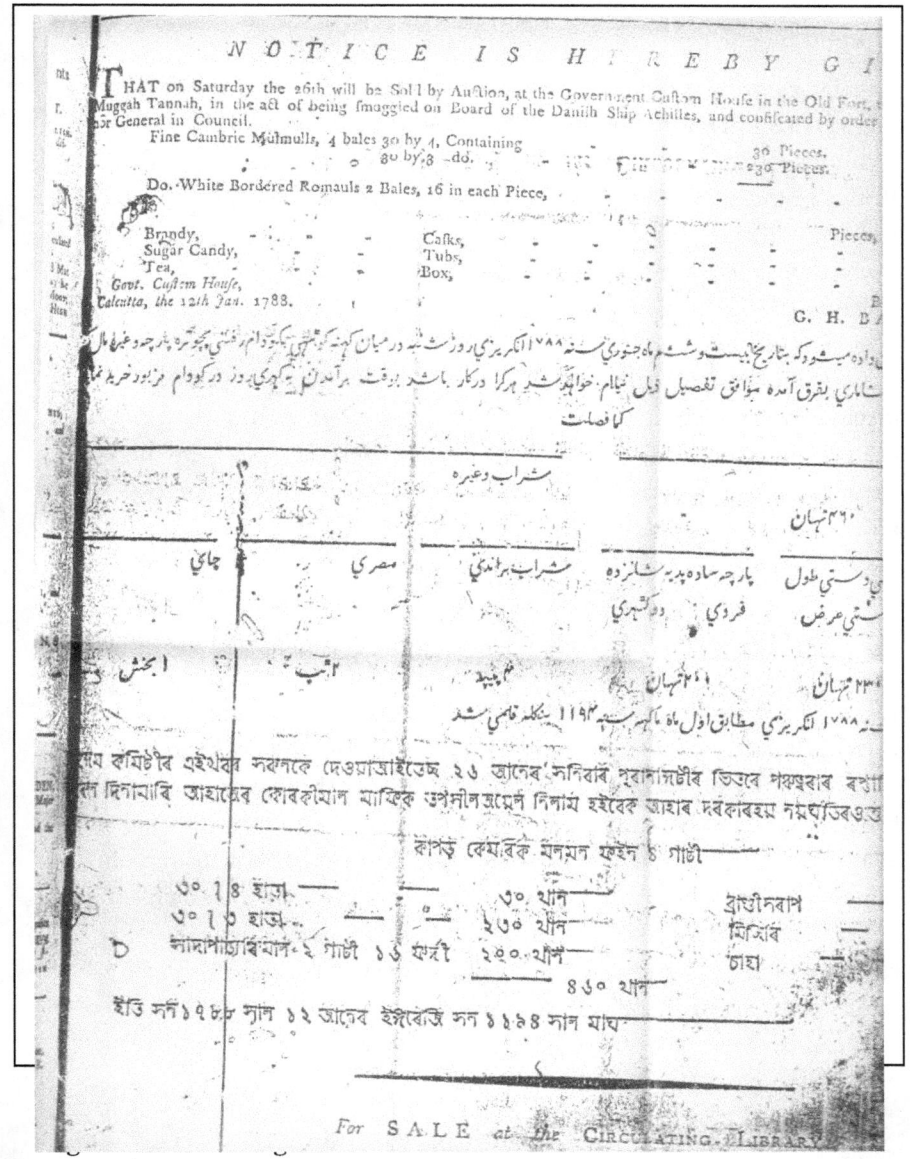

Conclusion.

Initially, all printing presses were owned by the British and all the printing presses that operated within Calcutta were imported from England. But the technology that was behind the printing press was never limited to the British printers; in fact, it was inevitable that each printing press would become a learning school for the natives. Local craftsmen, carpenters and blacksmiths were needed for maintenance and repair work. In "The Calcutta Press," J. H. Stocqueler states that the European printers would have had Indian compositors.[29] What this implies is that the European printers unwittingly taught a new generation of indigenous printers. An instance of how letterpress technology was transferred from the English to the Indians is evident in the manner in which Bengali types were made by Charles Wilkin, an employee of the East India Company. Wilkins was assisted by a native blacksmith, Panchanan Karmakar, who excelled his master in the art. It is difficult to cut the Bengali font, when compared to the Roman font, as the Bengali script has over six hundred symbols. Improvements were made to the Bengali font, and by 1785, the Honourable Company's Press was formed, from which emerged a set of Bengali books. *Regulations for the Administration of Justice in the Courts of Dewanee Adaulut* (1785), *Bengal Translation of Regulations for the Administration of Justice in the Fouzdarry or Criminal Courts: in Bengal, Behar, Orissa* (1791) were the first books of the press.[30] It was inevitable that the realm of power would shift. The Europeans knew the art of print, and the natives learnt from them. The imperatives for starting printing presses were largely due to certain governmental educational policies and missionary zeal. Whatever the reason, it eventually created a realm of native readership that became familiar with the materiality and conventions of print.

---

[29] J.H. Stoqueler, "The Calcutta Press," in *Calcutta Quarterly Magazine and Review* 3(Oct. 1833): 424-425.

[30] One of the first books to be printed in Calcutta was Nathaniel Brassey Halhed's *Grammar of the Bengal Language* in 1778, where the author draws attention to the mechanical aspects of print technology. The book was printed in a press established by Mr. Andrews, a book seller.

The emergence of early newspaper print in colonial Calcutta.

3 HOW NATIVES LEARNT ABOUT PRINT.

By the early nineteenth century, the realm of imperial print worked contiguously with the realm of native print. There was close intimacy between the Britishers and the natives -- an intimacy that did not operate on dislike, oppression or contempt. Natives were involved in the imperial realm of print as compositors, writers, booksellers, printers, teachers and translators, mastering and replicating all aspects of print culture and technology. It was almost as if the Britishers had on display the best of their culture so that the Indians would want to emulate them – which they did. It is not an exaggeration to say that Rammohun Roy was the first native to understand what it meant to participate in the newly established English print communication circuit – by engaging with English printers, starting his own printing house, and mastering the English language and the technology of print culture.

Literary writings and journals sprung up within the realm of imperial print in the late eighteenth century, and a sphere of literary-ness was cultivated within the colonial situation. It was easy for a Britisher raised in England to arrive in India and write literary works which were meant to be read by his fellow citizens in this part of the world. What would it have taken for a native to have access to this literary realm in Calcutta and if so, how would he have been trained? Henry Derozio was the first native who was able to engage with this realm of imperial literary print that had sprung up. While at Hindu College, he would have worked alongside someone like D.L. Richardson, who was also a teacher there, besides being a poet and an editor of the *Bengal Annual* - a yearly collection of poetry and prose that was published seven times between 1830 and 1836. Richardson was an active participant in the realm of imperial literary print, and Derozio would have had access to it through him. Henry Derozio published his first collection called *Poems* in 1827; the Baptist Mission Press in Srirampur was his publishing house. The same press published one of Rammohun Roy's initial works in 1819, *A Second Conference Between an Advocate and an Opponent on the Practice of Burning Widows Alive*. Everybody in the domain of English print knew each other. It was, after all, a small realm of print. The Mission Press was run by a group of European missionaries who were deeply involved with the realm of native print, and were also involved in printing books that were not meant for proselytisation. Indian pandits (like Ramram Basu, Chandicharan Munshi, Rajiblochan Mukhopadhay) attached to the Baptist Mission Press also printed books of fiction in Bengali, and can thus be described as the first writers in Bengali who had their works printed. A few decades previously, this same group of pandits would have used manuscripts, but now were turning their efforts to print technology, working alongside Christian missionaries and the officials of the East India Company.

In determining the nature of the new public work place that was established in the realm of the printing presses, we see that there would have been close physical contact between the Britishers and the Indians. Oftentimes, Indians worked as compositors in foundries which printed English works, without knowing the language. John Borthwick Gilchrist in his preface to *A Dictionary English and Hindoostanee*, wrote in 1798 that he was astounded with the "eternal treacherous behavior: of his Bengali assistants, a "posse of unprincipled black knaves."[31] H goes on to write about the "slavish drudgery of correcting the press ... where the compositors were every one more ignorant than another of the subject they were engaged to[*sic*]."[32] A similar shift occurred in Europe, in the modern period, with the introduction of printing presses where diverse occupational groups worked with each other in the new workshops that were set up by the early printers. Elisabeth Eisenstein describes the numerous processes that were involved: "The advent of printing led to the creation of a new kind of shop structure; to a regrouping which entailed closer contacts among diversely skilled workers and encouraged new forms of cross-cultural interchange." Thus it was not uncommon to find university professors and "former priests among early printers or former abbots serving as editors or correctors," thus, coming into closer contact with

---

[31] John Borthwick Gilchirst, *A Dictionary of English and Hindoostanee*. Printed by Stuart and Cooper, p. xv.

[32] Ibid, pp. xv, xii.

metal workers and mechanics.[33] When the printing presses were introduced in Bengal, the hierarchy between the English and the Indians was maintained. The editors and the master printers were Europeans, many of whom were employed from England, while the compositors were Indians.

The development of the realm of print culture in Calcutta and its subsequent use by the natives is an interesting story; as engaging and intriguing as the development of the city itself. The exchange that took place, albeit forced, coerced and under circumstances that were far from agreeable from the perspective of the natives, can also be described as a socio-cultural and technological engagement. For example, a few of the British printers who came to Calcutta had served as apprentices in England. George Gordon was the nephew of one of the most eminent eighteenth century London printers, William Strahan, who was the King's Printer, and a friend of Samuel Johnson and Benjamin Franklin. Most of them, though, were trained in Calcutta and a few can be named: Andrew Bones, Joseph Cooper, Paul Ferris, James Hicky, Thomas Jones, James Leary, Bernard Messink, John Miller, Aaron Upjohn, Charles Wilkins.[34] Eventually, it did not matter. The Europeans settled in India and introduced certain institutions and systems of rule and governance, both for themselves and for the natives. The realm of print was one such institution. Gradually, the Indians learnt it, and replicated all aspects of print. This process of cultural transmission and exchange did not pass through any phase of mimicry. What did matter was that the realm of print allowed both Britishers and the natives to engage with each other and for the natives, to reach out to a global readership.

---

[33] Elizabeth Eisenstein, "Defining the Initial Shift: Some Features of Print Culture" in *The Book History Reader*, ed. David Finkelstein and Alistair McCleery (London and New York: Routledge, 2002), pp. 156-157.

[34] For more see Graham Shaw, *Printing in Calcutta to 1800*, pp. 42-71.

4 SOME CONCLUDING THOUGHTS ON THE REALM OF EARLY PRINT.

Involving people and technology: the processes behind the creation of native fonts.

In a succinct commentary on how it took centuries for print to develop in the west, unlike the rapid fashion in how it evolved in Calcutta, Halhed, in *The Grammar of the Bengal Language*, summarizes the efforts taken by Charles Wilkins to perfect the native types:

> With a rapidity unknown in Europe, he surmounted all the obstacles which necessarily clog the first rudiments of a difficult art, as well as the disadvantages of solitary experiment; and has thus singly on the first effort exhibited his work in a state of perfection which in every part of the world has appeared to require the united the united improvements of different projectors, and the gradual polish of successive ages.

When the East India Company government established its printing press, Wilkins was its first head. But as we look closely at the nitty gritty details of the workings of the Srirampur Mission Press, one realizes that natives were active participants in the process of how technology was exchanged; Joshua Marshman, while describing Panchanan's efforts, wrote: "[with his] assistance we created a letter foundry, and although he is dead now, he had so full communicated his art to a number of others, that they carry forward the work of type casting, and even of cutting the matrices with a degree of accuracy which would not disgrace European artists."[35] Largely due to the efforts of William Carey, there was interaction between the Srirampur Mission press and the College of Fort William and many of the books written by the scholars of the college were printed in this press. Carey

---

[35] Nair, p. 96.

appointed many good scribes in different languages. The Bengali letters were engraved on the basis of a sample prepared by Kali Kumar Ray, the Bengali copyist of the College. Kali Kumar Ray must have been a scribe. What is interesting is that both natives and Englishmen were involved in the process of making types, therefore making the evolution of Indian print a collaborative venture.[36]

Panchanan taught the art of cutting types to Manohar, who was to become his son in law. Marshman described Manohar as "an expert and elegant workman who was subsequently employed for forty years at the Srirampur Press and to whose exertions and instructions Bengal is indebted for the various beautiful fonts of the Bengali, Nagree, Persian, Arabic and other characters which have been gradually introduced into the different printing establishments."[37] Over a span of around thirty years, between 1801-1830, the Srirampur Mission press printed books in over fifty languages.

A lot of intellectual labor went into the process of making types and perfecting the font. John Gilchrist made some changes to the printing of the Perso-Arabic scripts. In 1802, he wrote to the College Council: "as the types and printing materials which Mr. Gladwin presented to College are probably the best now to be procured, I request you will state to College my wish to take charge of, and employ them for the good of my department here, in the works I am about to publish in Hindoostanee language."[38] He also promised to return the types when needed to the College Council and thus was started the Hindoostane Press. Till that time period, there had been some presses in operation: the Chronicle Press, Stuart and Cooper Press, Ferris and Greenway Press, and the Hurkaru Press. On 20th June,

---

[36] Even though there were attempts to dismiss the natives involved, such an act did not take place. A letter in *The Annals* draws attention to this: "Many learned Natives are now attached to the Institution, who have been invited to Fort William by my special authority from different parts of Asia. ... The sudden dismission of the learned Natives attached to the College would therefore be an act of manifest injustice on the grounds already stated; it would also be an act of the most flagrant impolicy; nor would it be consistent either with the interest or the honour of the Company in India, ..."(l-li).

[37] Quoted in Nair, p. 97.

[38] Ibid., p. 98.

Gilchirst wrote to the College Council that he had made major improvements in 'Oriental typography' on the "European principle of separating words by spaces and joining the letters of each vocable, as much as possible." Lumsden subsequently made changes to Gilchrist's innovations. In 1805, he presented plans of improving the existing types in Persian and for establishing a new press. He also wanted a new set Persian types to be made by the best artists in Calcutta, under the guidance of Sheikh Kutb Ali, the Persian writing master at the College. He argued that "the letters of the Persian alphabet are joined together in such a manner as to render the frequent use of Logographic types indispensably necessary to the accurate execution of any literary work that may be printed in the Persian character."[39] The types that were used by the College were meant to "imitate more nearly the written character" and it was hoped that the press would vie with "manuscripts in beauty and cheapness" even it surpassed manuscripts in "accuracy."[40] The types were executed under the immediate supervision of natives attached to the College.[41]

It is not surprising that there are detailed discussions on the painstaking efforts taken to create the new types for Indian languages, and the sheer beauty of these native mechanical fonts. The emphasis was on the mechanical superiority of print versus handwritten manuscripts and to understand the logic of this argument, one needs to remember that by the end of the eighteenth century, when the socio-cultural characteristics of print were carried alongside the technology of print itself, print culture was seen at the apex of the communication circuit in Europe. Print technology in Europe during the fifteenth and sixteenth centuries reflected the larger social shift that was taking place whereby handicraft productions were giving way to mechanical processes and scribes were being replaced.[42] For this change to occur, a fundamental shift had to take place where printed

---

[39] Nair, p. 99.

[40] *Annals*, p. 210.

[41] Ibid., p. 211.

[42] Eisenstein, pp. 50-51, 54-55.

The emergence of early newspaper print in colonial Calcutta.

books were construed as more credible than manuscripts; printers thus started to champion the superior accuracy and credibility of books in comparison to manuscripts at the beginning of the sixteenth century.[43] There was nothing intrinsic to the trustworthiness of books, and in fact, Adrian Johns argues that when printed books were first published in the early modern period, textual corruptions multiplied; but this time period also saw printed texts as being socially constructed as more fixed and credible in comparison to handwritten texts.[44]

Within the colonial context in Calcutta, when we look closely at the debates and rationale raised on how the realm of print was to emerge, the concerns were not merely with replacing manuscript culture, but there was an equally strong emphasis on how beautiful the natives types were. Halhed, in the "Introduction" to the *Grammar of the Bengal Language* wrote on the mechanical aspects of the fonts:

> The public curiosity must be strongly excited by the beautiful characters which are displayed in the following work: and although my attempt may be deemed incompleat or unworthy of notice, the book itself will always bear an intrinsic value, from its containing as extraordinary an influence of mechanic abilities as has perhaps ever appeared. That the Bengal letter is very difficult to be imitated in steel will readily be allowed by every person who shall examine the intricacies of the strokes, the unequal length and size of the characters, and the variety of their positions and combinations. It was no easy task to procure a writer accurate enough to prepare an alphabet of a similar and proportionate body throughout, and with that symmetrical exactness which is necessary to the regularity and neatness of a fount.[45]

---

[43] Adrian Johns, *The Nature of the Book: Print and Knowledge in the Making.*. (Chicago: University of Chicago Press, 2000), p. 5.

[44] Ibid., p.31.

[45] Halhed. p. xxiii.

The element of beauty involved in the creation of the types in Indian languages is a factor that has never been considered in how print was construed in Europe. In many ways, such a perspective compels us to be more nuanced in how empire worked in the colonial context, legitimizing the need to invest time, labour, money and people in establishing a realm of print.

The emergence of early newspaper print in colonial Calcutta.

Works Cited:

Anderson, Benedict. *Imagined Communities: reflections on the origin and spread of nationalism*. (New York: Verso, 1991).

"Art. V. - On the effect of the Native Press in India," *The Friend of India*. Quarterly Series (No. 1): 130-154, pp. 132-133.

Atherton, Ian. "The Itch grown a Disease: Manuscript Transmission of news in the Seventeenth century" in Joan Raymond (ed.), *News, Newspaper and Society in Early Modern Britain* (London: Frank Cass, 1999), pp. 39-65.

Benedict, Barbara. *Readers, Writers, Reviewers and the Professionalization of Literature*. (Cambridge: Cambridge University Press, 2006).

Darnton, Robert. "What is the History of Books," *The Book History Reader*. ed. David Finkelstein and Alistair McCleery. (London and NY: Routledge, 2003), pp. 9-26.

Eisenstein, Elizabeth. "Defining the Initial Shift: Some Features of Print Culture" in *The Book History Reader,* ed. David Finkelstein and Alistair McCleery (London and New York: Routledge, 2002), pp. 156-157.

Gilchrist, John Borthwick. *A Dictionary of English and Hindoostanee*. Printed by Stuart and Cooper.

Halhed, Nathaniel. *A Grammar of the Bengal Language*, 1778. Reprint, ed. R. C. Alston (England: The Scolar Press, 1969).

Jones, Adrian. *The Nature of the Book: Print and Knowledge in the Making*. Chicago: University of Chicago Press, 2000.

Nair, Thankappan. *A History of the Calcutta Press*. (Calcutta: KLM Firma, 1987).

"Review of Halhed's *Grammar of the Bengal Language*," *The English Review, or, An Abstract of English and Foreign Literature* 1(1783): 5-14.

Shaw, Graham. *Printing in Calcutta to 1800* (London: The Bibliographical

Society, 1981).

Stoqueler, J.H. "The Calcutta Press," in *Calcutta Quarterly Magazine and Review* 3(Oct. 1833): 424-425.

The Annals of the College of Fort William, from the Period of its Foundation. Arranged and Published by Thomas Roebuck, Calcutta, Printed by Philip Periera at the Hindoostanee Press, 1819.

www.ingramcontent.com/pod-product-compliance
Lightning Source LLC
Chambersburg PA
CBHW071802040426
42446CB00012B/2680